A First Book of
CHOPIN

For the Beginning Pianist

with Downloadable MP3s

by
Bergerac

DOVER PUBLICATIONS
Garden City, New York

All songs available as downloadable MP3s!

Go to: http://www.doverpublications.com/0486424278
to access these files.

For Nicole

Biographical Note

A First Book of Chopin for the Beginning Pianist with Downloadable MP3s is a new work, first published by Dover Publications in 2003.

The quotation on contents page 3 is an excerpt from a contemporary concert review reprinted in the Chopin Biography in Volume 4 of *The New Grove Dictionary of Music and Musicians,* © Maxmillan Publishers Limited, 1980. The quotations included in the headings of pages 20 and 22 are taken from David Dubal's *The Art of the Piano,* copyright © 1995, 1989 by David Dubal, published by Harcourt Brace & Company, Orlando, Florida.

Chopin's image on the cover and page 3 reproduces an authentic painting of the young composer. The artist is unknown.

International Standard Book Number

ISBN-13: 978-0-486-42427-9
ISBN-10: 0-486-42427-8

Manufactured in the United States of America
42427815   2022
www.doverpublications.com

Frédéric Chopin

"Chopin knows what sounds are heard in our fields and woods," wrote a critic. "He has listened to the song of the Polish villager, and he has made it his own." But the composer's adopted France brought a new elegance and refinement into his music, and Frédéric Chopin, revered as "the poet of the piano," was welcomed into Paris's highest social and courtly circles. The story and music of a great composer forever torn between two worlds appear in the pages that follow.

Contents

In approximate order of difficulty

Italian words in this music, and what they mean

Allegretto = play at a moderately quick, light tempo

Allegro con brio = play fast, with excitement

Andante = play at a "walking" speed (*andare* means "to walk")

Andantino = play at a speed that's slightly faster and lighter than *Andante*

a tempo = return to the original speed

Cantabile = songful

cresc. (crescendo) poco a poco = get louder little by little

crescendo e allargando = get louder and hold back the speed

D.C. al Fine [da capo al fine] = literally, "from the head to the tail"; that is, go back to the beginning, then continue to the word "Fine" (end)

dolce = sweetly, gently

espr. (espressivo) = expressive

espr., sost. (espressivo, sostenuto) = expressive, sustained

Fine = the end

Largo = play at a very slow tempo

legato = connect the notes in a smooth way

Lento = play slowly

Maestoso = play at a majestic, broad speed

marcato = marked, accented

Moderato cantabile = play at a moderate speed, and in songful way

molto legato = very smoothly connected

poco accel. (accelerando) = speed up a little

poco rall. (rallentando) = hold back a little

poco rit. (ritardando) = slow down a little

rall. (rallentando) = hold back your speed

rall. (rallentando) molto = hold back a lot

rall. (rallentando) poco a poco = hold back little by little

rit. (ritardando) = slow down

Semplice = play in a simple, unaffected way

sempre stacc. (staccato) = always detached

sost. (sostenuto) = sustained, connected

sostenuto e cantabile = sustained and songful

sotto voce = hushed (literally, "in an under voice")

An Elegant Chopin Melody

(in French Ballroom Style)

The seventh Prelude from Chopin's 24 Preludes, Op. 28, composed when he was 26. The music is really a delicate waltz, made up of rhythmically identical two-measure phrases. Originally in the key of A major, this version states the melody alone in the easier key of G major, then adds a simple bass line. The music is light, airy and elegant. Play it at an easy-going walking speed.

A Plaintive Chopin Melody

(in Polish *Mazurka* Style)

The middle section of the Mazurka in G minor, Op. 67 no. 2, composed the year Chopin died. This is a song full of longing for his homeland, Poland. A sad tune, played quietly, as though lost in thought about times past. Our version is a whole-step higher than the original, played in the key of A minor.

Lullaby

The theme of Chopin's *Berceuse* [bear-SIRS], Op. 57, originally in D-flat major and in 6/8. Here in G major, our notation in 3/4 is much easier to play, yet captures the original feeling. Since Chopin never married and had no children, it is not surprising that this lullaby is the only composition of this sort among his works. (Compare this to music by his contemporary Robert Schumann, who had a huge family and wrote many piano pieces for, and about, his children.) >

Gently, with a quiet rocking motion

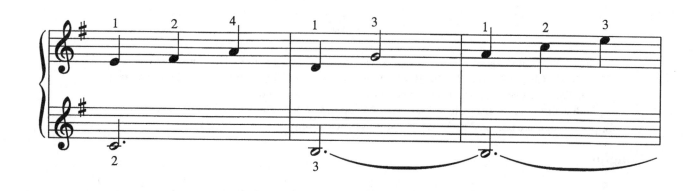

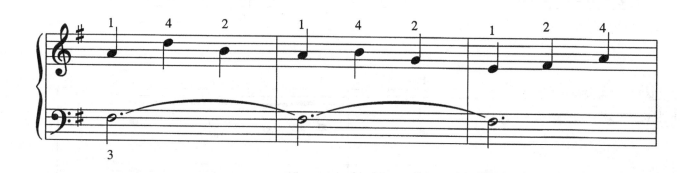

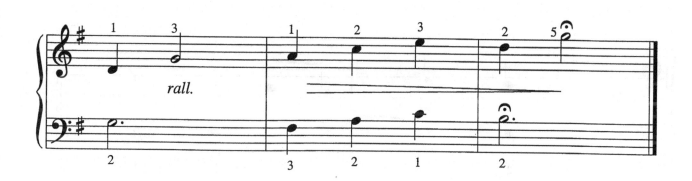

Mazurka

The main theme of Chopin's Mazurka, Op. 67 no. 2—a different section of the music on page 7 ("A Plaintive Chopin Melody"). The Mazurs were country folk living near Warsaw, the capital of Poland. The *mazurka* [mah-ZOOR-kah], one of their popular national dances, was known as early as the 16th century, and was a particular favorite of Chopin, who wrote more than 60 of these dances for piano. Some are bold and lively; others, plaintive and dreamy.

Songful

a tempo

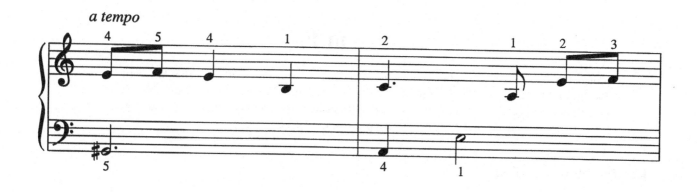

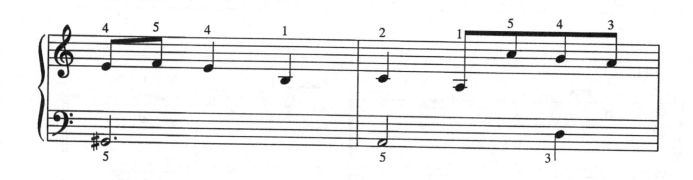

gradually slower

Mazurka in F

Chopin's Op. 68 no. 3, composed when he was 19, but not published until 20 years after his death at the age of 39. Here's a totally different face for the mazurka: this time it's a jaunty, light-hearted, and very youthful dance piece—the exact opposite of the plaintive mazurka on page 10. As you play, picture the bright, heel-tapping movement of happy, young dancers.

Lively, but not too fast

poco rall.

Etude No. 3

The Etude in E major, Op. 10 no. 3, originally in 2/4. This version in F major presents one of Chopin's most beautiful melodies, known all over the world for its lovely simplicity. Since *étude* [AYE-tood] means "a study," this famous piece seems to be Chopin's study in a full, "singing" tone at the keyboard, with a gently rocking accompaniment in the left hand. Our version in 4/4 doubles all the original note values (quarters instead of 8ths) for easier reading.

Gently, but not too slow

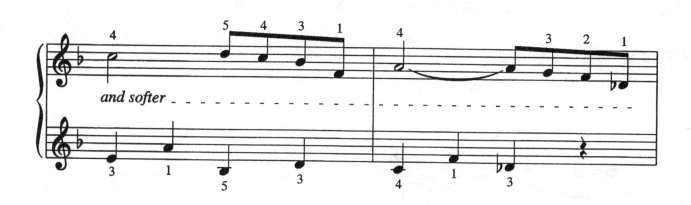

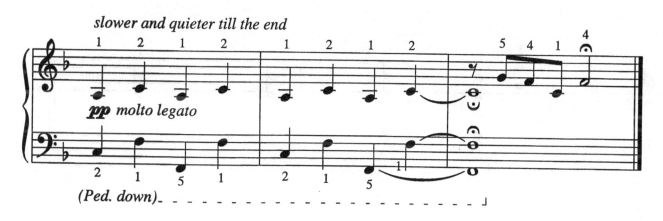

Prelude No. 7

A complete version of the gentle French waltz introduced on page 6. Among Chopin's works, the title "Prelude" has no special meaning. Of his 24 pieces with this title, some are sketches barely a minute long; others are quite developed and theatrical. With its two-measure rhythm played *eight* times, Prelude No. 7 presents a challenge to shape the music in an interesting way, with varying "dynamics" (degrees of loud and soft) as you move from phrase to phrase.

Andantino

An Early Nocturne

The theme of the famous Nocturne in E-flat, Op. 9 no. 2 (here, in G major), composed when the frustrated and disappointed 20-year-old Chopin was still unknown to the music world. The title "nocturne"—meaning "night piece"— however, was invented by composer-pianist John Field, an Irishman almost 30 years older than Chopin. But it was Chopin who captured the world's attention with 21 magnificent nocturnes composed over the last dozen years of his life.

Slowly flowing

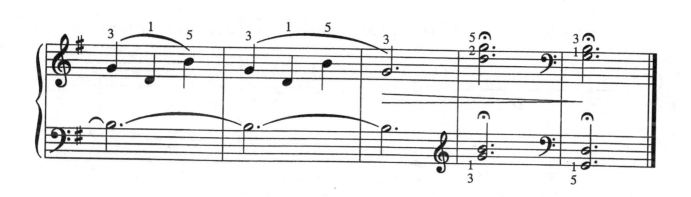

A Late Nocturne

The Nocturne, Op. 55 no. 1, originally in F minor, now a whole-step higher, in G minor. Chopin's nocturnes have been called "love poems of the finest ardor, and within each one an intimate human drama is explored." As you learn this sweet-sad music, what do *you* hear? What "story" may be hidden behind those eloquent melodies? (Or is there no story at all?)

Andante

(omit this note on the final repeat)

poco rall.

1st and Last ending

2nd time   *a tempo*

Stop here after the final repeat.

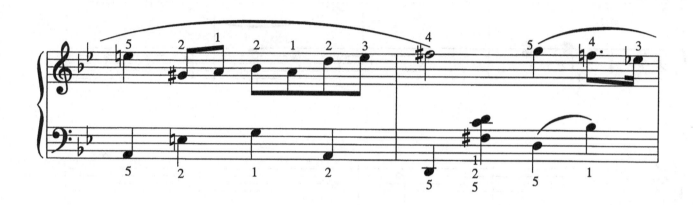

gradually held back before the main theme returns _ _ _ _ _ _ _ _ _ _ _ _

First Ballade

The lyrical slow theme from Ballade No. 1 in G minor, Op. 23, here in C major. Some say that this is the work that awakened the music world to the genius of young Frédéric Chopin. Listen to a recording of the original piece if you can: This perfect blend of heart-melting poetry and electrifying power has been called a "glowing masterpiece." 1

Flowing and songful

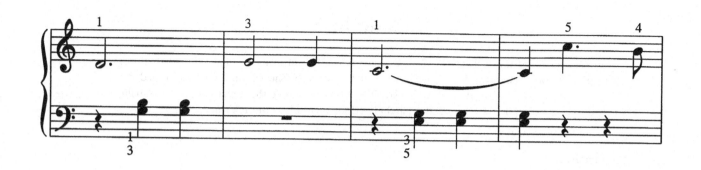

gradually held back until the end

(freely, slowly)

Ballade in F

The main theme of the Ballade No. 2 in F major, Op. 38, still in its original key and rhythms. Composer Robert Schumann had dedicated one of *his* pieces to Chopin. So Frédéric returned the favor by dedicating this Ballade to *him*. Today, it seems unbelievable that great composers actually talked to each other, had dinner together, and played for each other! But it's true.

Andantino

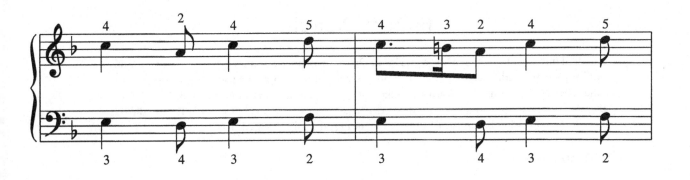

rall. _ _ _ _ poco _ _ _ _ a _ _ _ _ poco

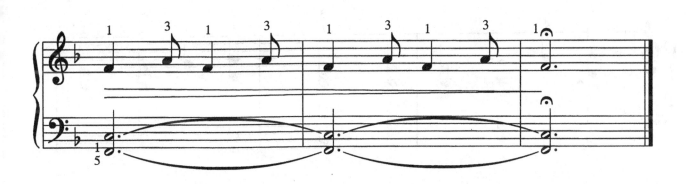

25

Funeral March

The third movement of Chopin's Sonata No. 2, Op. 35. Despite the tempo marking, don't drag this familiar piece to death! Keep the rhythm steady, moving along at a gentle pace. Notice that the left hand *never* changes; once you learn the fingering, you've got nothing more to think about! Then give some shape to the music: perhaps it could start and end very softly, but build in the middle—as though the procession began far, far away, came nearer, then disappeared.)

Slow and heavy

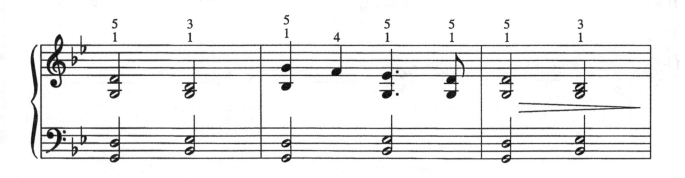

gradually dying away till the end

Mazurka in C

The original theme, key, and rhythms of the Mazurka, Op. 33 no. 3. This is our first piece to include a large number of *grace notes*—those quick, little decorations written in very small notes. *Grace notes have no time value*, so don't let them stick out! Instead, play them with light fingers, just a split-second before the beat. The result will be charming, fanciful dance rhythms.

Semplice

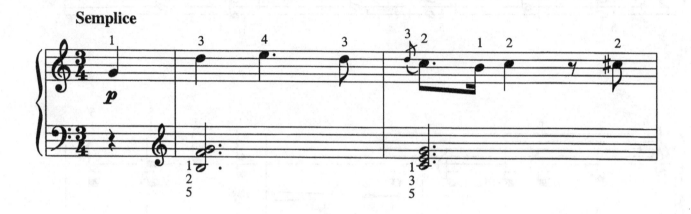

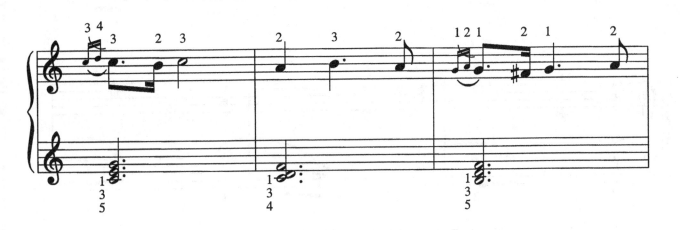

Grand Waltz in A Minor

The theme of the Grande Valse Brillante, Op. 34 no. 2. Close your eyes and imagine Paris, the most beautiful and fashionable city in all of Europe. Picture a candle-lit ballroom, music in the air, and elegant dancers in fine dress. Yet underneath it all is a hint of melancholy and sweet sadness. Was young Chopin thinking of his Polish homeland as he composed this quiet piece?

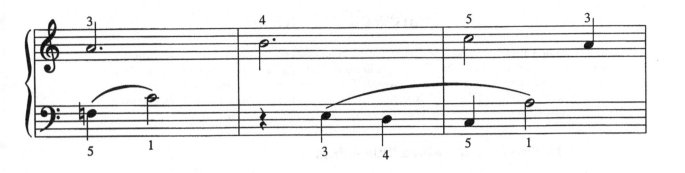

rall. _ _ _poco _ _ _a _ _ _poco

D.C. al Fine

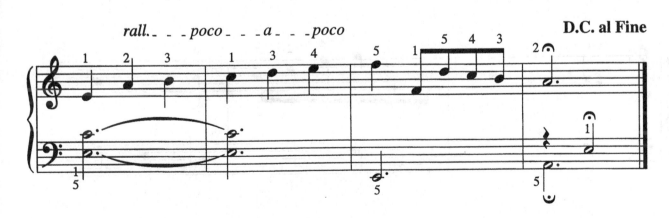

"Farewell" Waltz

The Waltz in A-flat, Op. 69 no. 1, called "L'adieu" (The Farewell). It is said that Chopin wrote this waltz while courting a young Polish countess living in Paris. But as a poor musician, he was considered unsuitable for marriage and was rejected. True or not, it is a romantic tale that perfectly fits the poetic 19th century. (Those 13 little notes at the 2nd ending, p. 33, are typical decorations in Chopin's style. Play the phrase lightly, as though you were throwing it away.)

Lento — quietly, with a little sadness

Play these 13 notes in an unhurried, smooth and even way.

"Minute" Waltz

The lyrical middle section of the world-famous Waltz in D-flat, Op. 64 no. 1. The misleading word "Minute" was probably the publisher's idea, for it surely did not come from a composer who disliked nicknames for his music. Although the main theme flows quickly, it takes far more than a minute to play this delightful waltz. The "free" 8th-note-passages that begin and end this three-page piece are from Chopin's original score. (Remember to turn after page 35.)

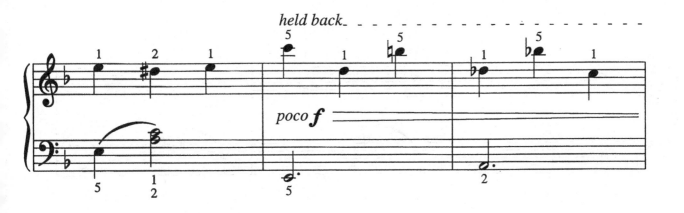

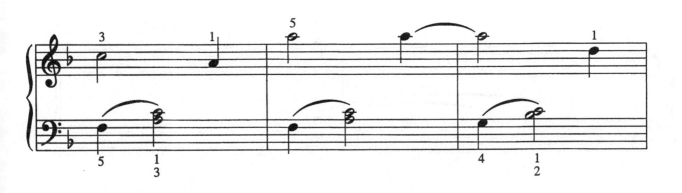

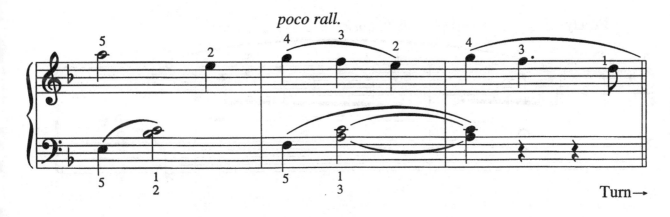

Turn→

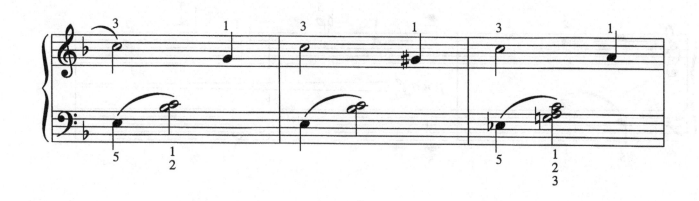

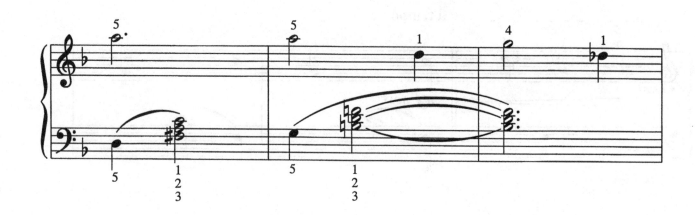

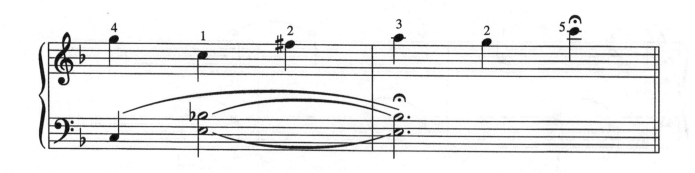

Freely _ _ _ _ _ _ _ _ _ _ _ *held back* _ _ _ _ _ _ _ _

"Organ" Prelude

The complete Prelude in C minor, Op. 28 no. 20, transposed to G minor. The nickname "Organ" captures the way this powerful miniature imitates thick organ sound by using a combination of rich chords (in the hands) and the damper pedal (with the foot) to make the lower piano strings resonate fully and deeply. Just strike each chord and hold it . . . then quickly depress and hold the right pedal until you play the next chord. Then do it again!

37

"Raindrop" Prelude

The theme of Prelude in D-flat, Op. 28 no. 15, here in D major. Those repeated A's in the left hand are supposed to imitate raindrops, but no one really knows what was on Chopin's mind when he composed this music. For the best performance, play that lovely right-hand melody very smoothly *(legato)* and sweetly *(dolce)*, while your left hand intones those A's in the background, quietly and lightly detached *(piano e poco leggiero)*. Practice hands separately!

Sostenuto

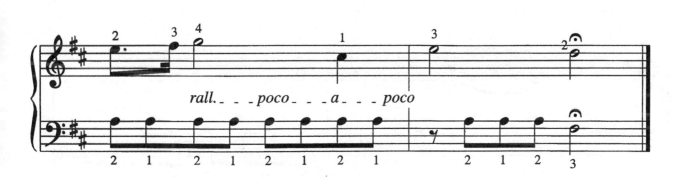

Fantaisie-impromptu

The slow theme—originally in D-flat major, here in F major, from the Fantaisie-impromptu, Op. 66. And what a beautifully balanced musical form!—16 measures altogether (count them) . . . perfectly divided into two pages . . . each page perfectly divided into four little phrases. As you play this world-famous music, listen to how effortlessly it unfolds . . . expands . . . repeats . . . and comes to rest.

Moderato cantabile

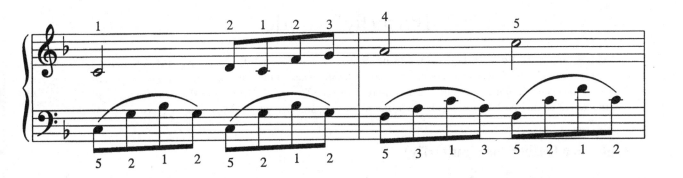

Notice that this left-hand passage is *identical* to measure 3 — but now in the bass clef.

rall. _ _ _ _ poco _ _ _ _ a _ _ _ _ poco

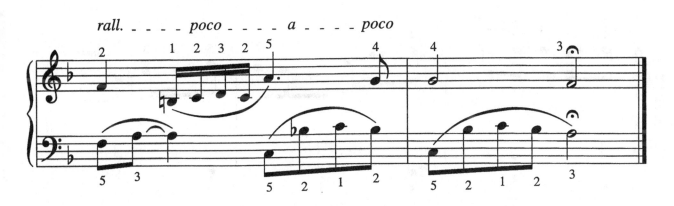

41

"Butterfly" Etude

The theme of the Etude in G-flat, Op. 25 no. 9. Every *étude* (French for "a study") has something special to teach the player. This one must be about lightness and a delicate touch in piano playing, for it just seems to fly along, soaring here and there with no effort at all. Remember that you are now in the key of C, that both hands are always in the treble clef, and that *pp* means *pianissimo* (very soft).

Light as a feather (or a butterfly)

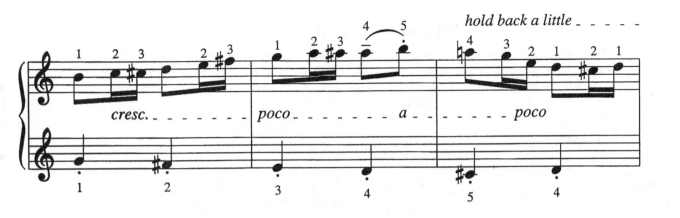

"Military" Polonaise

What began as a peasant song-and-dance in Poland's villages soon reached the great reception halls of high society, where splendidly dressed guests pranced in courtly processionals to the spirited martial music of their country. This was the famous *polonaise*—the highest expression of Polish national spirit. But it remained for Frédéric Chopin to elevate the polonaise to its highest form, making these piano works a symbol to all the world of intense Polish nationalism.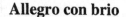

Allegro con brio

Fine

a tempo

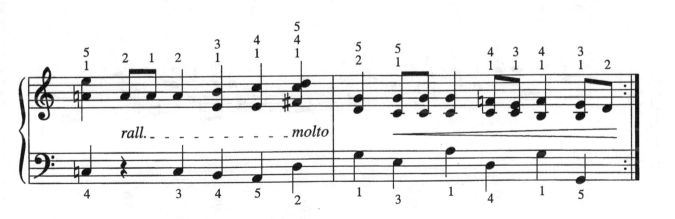

"Heroic" Polonaise

It was 1830, and the unknown Chopin (just turned 20) had left Poland for the first time to seek fame in Europe's musical world. He was performing in Stuttgart, Germany, when he learned of the capture of Warsaw by the Russians under Csar Nicolas I. Chopin's dream of a free, all-powerful Poland never left him, finding intense expression in his two most famous works: the "Military" Polonaise (Op. 40 no. 1) and this driving, emotional "Heroic" Polonaise (Op. 53).

46

Scottish Dance

The first of three *Écossaises*, Op. 72 no. 3. In French, "Scotland" is *Écosse*, and a "Scottish dance" is *écossaise*. Published after Chopin's death, this music was written when the composer was barely 16 years old. It is carefree and jolly, full of youthful good spirits—a pleasant way to end our musical visit with this complex, emotional composer whose heart never left home.

Lively, with bright spirits